Again

AGAIN

POEMS 1989-2000

Joanne Kyger

LA ALAMEDA PRESS   ALBUQUERQUE

Some of these poems have appeared in
New Censorship, Make Way for Da-Da, Gas Magazine,
Mike & Dale's Younger Poets, Gare du Nord, Gate, Penumbra,
Melancholy Breakfast, Aljadid, The Real News (online
chapbook at *Big Bridge*), *Some Life* (Post-Apollo Press),
and *From Joanne Kyger* (Longhouse).

front cover:
Apsaras are flying celestial nymphs in Indian mythology,
divinities of water & clouds, and experts at converting ascetics
through their beauty. The Buddhist temple caves at Dunhuang
on China's Silk Road have thousands of dancing apsaras brightly
painted on the grotto walls and ceilings. "The maidens hold
musical instruments tied with colorful ribbons and spread
flower blossoms like rain drops over the world."
These are a detail from a gilt bronze standard—
Asuka Period (seventh century A.D.) Japan
Tokyo National Museum

ISBN: 1-888809-25-6

Library of Congress Control #: 2001 132058

La Alameda Press
9636 Guadalupe Trail NW
Albuquerque, New Mexico 87114

BOOKS BY JOANNE KYGER

The Tapestry and The Web (Four Seasons Foundation, 1965)

The Fool in April: A Poem (Coyote Books, 1966)

Joanne (Angel Hair Books, 1970)

Places to Go (Black Sparrow Press, 1970)

Desecheo Notebook (Arif Press, 1971)

Trip Out and Fall Back (Big Sky, 1975)

Lettre de Paris / with Larry Fagin
(Poltroon Press, 1977)

The Wonderful Focus of You (Z Press, 1980)

Japan and India Journals, 1969-1964
with photographs by Gary Snyder and Allen Ginsberg
(Tomboctou Books, 1981)

Mexico Blondé (Evergreen Press, 1981)

Up My Coast
adapted from the stories of
C. Hart Merriam; illustrated by Inez Storer
(Floating Island Books, 1981)

Going On: Selected Poems 1958-1980 (Dutton, 1983)

The Dharma Committee (Smithereens Press, 1986)

Man-Woman / with Michael Rothenberg
illustrated by Nancy Davis (Big Bridge Press, 1988)

Phenomenological (Institute of Further Studies, 1989)

Just Space: Poems 1979-1990
illustrated by Arthur Okamura
(Black Sparrow Press, 1991)

Some Sketches from the Life of Helena Petrovna Blavatsky
(Rodent Press, 1996)

Pátzcuaro (Blue Millennium Press, 1999)

Some Life (Post-Apollo Press, 2000)

Selected Works (Penguin, 2001) forthcoming

Contents

Again

Life has a repetitious feel,
continuing the yearly progression of one's history
          in one place
     change is subtle, sometimes hardly noticed
and then a large gasp, someone is gone, forever.

     The migrating flocks return
the coast range changes color,
  monarchs come back . . .
     'restless surface watching the minutes'

     Not too much happens   strands
          of consciousness,   strands of dreams
               precious, rare and mundane, where we live

Haven't I seen you
here before?

That's me!
When I began.

1989

Anthro Info

The Immortals   are so old
you can't remember
when you first started remembering them

1989

Incense for the Buddha

Boy do I burn
a lot & that's about All
I do.

OCTOBER 24, 1989

Friday 2:44 PM

The sun is about to pass
    from behind the last tree
    in the eucalyptus grove   Soon in a few
more minutes maybe five
              to spend gazing at the wild ruffle
      of scrofularia, coyote bush, coffee berry
                Just waiting, & waiting
          to finish and lie down
again while the sun keeps its downward path
           before drowning off Agate Beach reef.

Chin in hand I see them bobbing along the surf line
    in tender dalliance
Lovely to remember while the westward orb silhouettes
      the sickle shaped leaves of the grove
    and we'll soon be eyeball to light
    soothing the musing of expectation —
It's here   the moment begins.

November 17, 1989

20

Cold
Full Moon
Restless
Fill up chattering monkey void with stories
    all night long, visit the Zen Center,
Swim in their pool. Do I have the lineage?
    When does the transmission come.

DECEMBER 12, 1989

Home

I am Home.
　　　　Getting here to escape
to a new floor plan
out of the chill of the day

Here World!　Here World!
(like Here Dog!　Here Dog!)

FEBRUARY 5, 1990
1:23 PM

Stew

California Lilac, Ceanothus, embraced
in the vase Frog holds looking upward
    at a reasonable hour
            about the last of them . . .
Possible to take care only   of what is local?
  Well, I AIN'T ART says Arthur Okamura
    referring to a much   too familiar nick-name.
Looking for genuine enthusiasm,
         spend only a day
OK, it's evening
     and the sun is softly leaving
    sky luminous rosy
It's pretty windy
    says Donald Guravich   coming from the northwest
  and looking towards the stew.

FEBRUARY 1990

You murmur   'Earth'
        What are you dreaming about?   'Corn'

Dreaming something a little deeper
The people are nicer
                to each other, there are adventures
        not melodramas
in the finely etched bubbles of the brain.

And you, friend, travel so much farther, soothing
        walks in Tamalpais's mist covered redwoods

A return to the continuous story.

                                MAY 21, 1990

24

In Memoriam

First, there were the FIRST PEOPLE
And then the First People made the ANIMALS
And then the ANIMALS made Our People

And this is Memorial Day   weekend with unusual
     rainy overcast skies,   tide the lowest
In twenty years causing the Agate Beach parking lot
     to overflow with cars and their human content
     visiting this Ocean withdrawal phenomena
   much advertised by the media.   Place to go to, Kids.
All camouflage revealed in air.   You know what I mean —
It's the littoral zone.   Where human feet can squish
   the living daylights out of cowering anemone
And the local boys can *walk* to the furthest reef pool
     pick up their abalone and go home.
     So far out, this a view to be seen
     inside the flight of 70 black brants that didn't
want to move,   they *didn't* want to move.

MAY 26, 1990

Some *Frivolity*

CRAZED THE BABY TAPE CASSETTE

DOESN'T WORK   NEW ONE WHAT IS WRONG
How did you get made
imperfect, struggling, out on the street.

Sounds like wrentit rattle
viceroy butterfly floats
actually flies
by indiscriminate to thoughts
like patty cake mud pies

Something completely and divinely enigmatic:
PLUG IT IN THE RIGHT HOLE!

Help me to perform the Turkey Breast Polka
now into deep address.
This is duty time.   Followed by ditties.
Oh give me a chance.

A lemon tart with tits
is how B described D
this morning. This morning is glorious!   Blonde
sunny, following last night's artistic endeavors.
An iridescent fly now.   Curly hair.
Distinctly piqued,   mostly graceful.

May 31, 1990

They are alive *although* celadon

The house is lightly lived in
     A lone celadon parrot
   sits in the front room
Later on the house looks deserted except
    for the silent celadon cat
  in the front window. I enter

because I must find a place to get my clothes
together
I am homeless
And my clothes need to be ironed, need to be groomed
 I do this quietly in the attached empty garage
   My clothes they need attention
The house looks moved out, abandoned

I open the garage door onto the street. Oh
    the man appearing in front of me
lives here. Anyway, I am brave.
I tell him the truth. I need a place
  A place to get my clothes my clothes
together. It looks empty except for the cat
But *he* lives here, *he* really lives here.

JUNE 2, 1990
FOR ALICE NOTLEY

Moments That Come

I am dancing around the plaza with a policeman
in a black leather suit.   It is the samba
and our dance
is easily coordinated.   He unzips his fly
   and has a small ejaculation performance
      in a nearby rest room involving a towel
         and a sink

Down in the underworld of poverty, the old dogs
   huskies,   newfoundlands,   large old shaggy dogs
      leftover purgatory   of animals.

            Well, this is a dream
      of animal spirits overbred, neglected
         and their keeper down there with them
in those cavernous tunnels and dens   Sleepy
   neglected   fat   but not dangerous for one
      who passes through softly
         on her journey.

June 6, 1990

'We are strong
        and vulnerable at the same time. Strength comes
    when we face the inevitability of our own death.
    When death comes there is no one to help you.
    There are no friends, no teachers, no kind words.
    There is just your awareness.'
                        — Osel Tenzin
                        formerly Thomas Rich
                        Vancouver November 12 '87
                Dharma heir of
        Chogyam Trungpa   who died
        on April 4, 1987.

                Osel Tenzin died yesterday
            August 25, 1990 at 9:05 PM of AIDS-related
    pneumonia. A short lineage.   He supposedly thought
        he was protected against illness.
                The 'organization' falters.
                    Was this a test?

                                AUGUST 26, 1990

29

Continuing Adventures in the Life of Naropa

So

he gets fired up and burnt up
he is in great pain

burnt out
nobody's home
nothing doing
okay
keep that vivid vivid   experience
alive

Commitment

'Oh teacher let me give you this bowl of food'
'It's delicious'
'Shall I get you some more?'
'Yes. Go ask for some more.'

So he does, and gets beat up.

No second helpings here.

SEPTEMBER 10 & 11, 1990

Part of My Seminal Ground Work

HELP
The gold crown song returned today
Spicy smell in a box I mean boxed in
Dongs of Gods   Dongs of Humans
This is the very best I can do
Achoo

SEPTEMBER 19, 1990

31

It Certainly Was Divine Running into You

Well, just a momentary good idea as your form

    changes so often I can't catch

                up to you *now*
        a large hawk sitting in the loquat tree close

    to the ground and then
        you are thunder growl borrowed from the northern

storms   on their way   in a day or two and leaves
        are bedding their ground around the buckeye

    The little chirruping flocks

    Kwan Yin Willow

             new moon
has hardly seemed   to grow

SEPTEMBER 25, 1990

Dried Shrimp

When no alternatives are left
    It's poetry
        the last resort

    Open your mouth
    Rosa es rosa es rosa

Who is that tapping on the window
      tapping on the door   near midnight
        Saturday night

And a bird appears in the dark kitchen
      Tuesday morning
Staying inside all day the withered limbs
    of otoño
        drop golden leaves

Good looking lizard
1910 Mexican Revolution

Guadalupe, scatter wild roses
    behind the door here
      where fire warms the room
      and the sun sets

over the mountains behind Pátzcuaro's lake
And our old father leaves us

NOVEMBER 14, 1990
PÁTZCUARO

Valentine

is flat on his back being hurt
by the bad back of burden.
                    So there is all
this pain hurtling toward
        some wisdom of compassion's drop off

A trap door suddenly opens to reveal a pit
of writhing octopus, good for you,
        says friendly Asian couple, good for you
to know you can eat
    drink and merry be damned into the dark night.

Pursued we reach the palm shaded courtyard
    and the young dark man draws
            his arrow at the white puma's heart
                    and they are really poised
there for a long time in this rendition
of spirit force.   Struggle to wake.

    So who do you go to

    for help in confusion,   seeing
what all humans see.
                    Hummingbird looking
            for nectar, dead flowers
        after frost.

FEBRUARY 14, 1991

Friday Night

        In pale blue dusk   sky   Moon
      is nice light gold.   Oh where
    are you going
  my favorite friends in a flock   Gold crown
song is going north
     for the summer   has different
   seeds up there   up there friend moon
is getting larger.

APRIL 26, 1991

A Story from Easter: *He Has Risen*

There is a mouse under the sink
Little mouse turds around in the kitchen drawers
It is raining, storming
The refrigerator
has gone to the dump
Donald's back
has brought him to bed for several months
He can't move
The war is skidding to an 'end'
Who wants to kill anything.
Buy two mousetraps
               and leave them   unset
around in conspicuous places
I think it's gone away.   One day
I take the peanut oil from under the sink
The top is gone.
Inside the peanut oil
is the body of a mouse.
Oh!   too horrible
Look   look at this!
I put it outside the back door
The top of the bottle is really very narrow
He wiggled in head first
He can't back out
He's drowned   but preserved
He's in his oil tomb for two weeks
On Easter day I look at the bottle.

He has risen
            to the top
Donald   now walks

Buries mouse next day.

APRIL 27, 1991

For Your Birthday, Philip

& upon the occasion of becoming
Abbot of the Hartford Street Zen Center
October 10, 1991

A superabundance, an excess, a plethora of greetings
                    May they shower down
                    like baby Peony
                    petals — but that's spring —
            Isn't it   the autumnal
            Imperial Kiku
          every year
                thinking of the chrysanthemums
                          Being thought of *by* them

            In the fall   here
          6000 feet up it's the quaking
        Aspen that turn gold
      Shimmering and trembling
                  among the steady green
              of fir mountain
      Who says you can't make a pond out of a bowl?
                I'd better stay and fill it up   Philip
                  For your Birthday   — Here!
              the many branches of this light
            purple chrysanthemum   You can read
                from this mind
                giving you on paper
                the faint crisp odor
                of time

A late October afternoon
and the mountains are slipped in snow
A gold leaf falls
It *is* fall
And those far off peaks shining
Pure and rare.

BOULDER, COLORADO
WITH SHIKI AND HAN YU
OCTOBER 20, 1991

On Moving to the Naropa Campus Fall 1991

This for the Tuesday morning
                    dreams
All the old friends
                    in new but familiar
Adventures

        Many many   a thousand
                hands in positions
        of compassionate
Awakening

            There *is* a plug
        for your electric
        toothbrush in the bathroom

            Snow
on the way   in the foothills.

Dharma: the suitcase of many meanings

Amid all the blood of illusion, eating roast chicken
           and hiding the eyes
           the rivulets of dreams pass on.
Earthquakes, landslides, rockfalls, ground subsidence,
           radioactive wastes.   All here
along the front range adding hazard to beauty.
           I think I   have too many clothes on.
And it is a beauteous evening, calm and fair with broad sun
           sinking behind the front range
           and the derangement of attire
           is reaping frustration for the pure soul
           whose heart is acceptable for naught
But cuts across the reflex of a star.

OCTOBER 18, 1991
BOULDER

41

Snow fall   on   green leaves
Eye is twitching quite dreadfully
I'm going to be cool
and soften the dreadful hate
and pity I have in my heart

October 28, 1991
Boulder

Love

When people say they love me I tell them
Give me a loaf of bread   — I loaf you!

Snow

I wish I could stop thinking of Robert
Frost whenever it snows

OCTOBER 1991
BOULDER

43

Oh the weather, the weather
Makes hectic stirrings inside
of me the drastic elements of fury
and calm drastic winds of change

NOVEMBER 7, 1991
BOULDER

Ooold Man Tolstoy

I need a bitter taste   a tonic
                                for Spring

   lightness

                        MARCH 1992

Ocean Parkway Gazing

Ocean up
against cliff
        Long thin roll
of surf over

    longest shale reef of the North Coast
and way out tiny point is buoy
        is light at night
        signaling danger
            But this morning is peaceful
                Just light
movement of breeze cool caress
    like a nursery song.
Flat glimmering gliding surface
    Past echium's purple plumes in hues
  spotted with bees
Catching a morning breakfast.

    The Coast Range rises light
        mossy green and in its folds
    dark design
            of fir, redwood and pine.
    Monarchs 'empower' this scene
                when they land
    lightly in their cruise
        for nectar.   Poison oak
    just a yard away.

    The voice describes the scene
        looks up for reference

    listens to two
      song sparrows carry out
their call

And response as the hissy light
      waves roll over changing continuum.
The minutes go by the sea
    The sea closes in
          Up to the edge
of mythology.

MARCH 17, 1992

II

Muso Soseki
companion on the bench
beside me
restless surface watching
the minutes, endless
silver inlets
down the coast

8:28 AM
MARCH 24, 1992

Specially
for Your Eyes

If you make it this far you are fairly out of danger
because now you are on foot
on dirt roads, edged with sunlight
and small birds.   When the wind
comes up you inhale it whole
and slowly distribute it
calm   the torrent of breathing

MARCH 30, 1992

49

Adonis is Older than Jesus

Ever heard of a place called Byblus?
An ancient place
with an ancient god
a great god
called   El

and where King Cinyras
father of Adonis
ruled

And Byblus remained
as religious capital
of the country

on a height
beside the sea

And further south
the River Adonis
falls   into   the sea
from its source on Mt Lebanon
a day's journey away

Oh the River Adonis
rushes from a cavern
'at the foot of a mighty amphitheater
of towering cliffs
to plunge in a series of cascades
into the depths of the glen.

The deeper it descends
the ranker and denser grows
the vegetation, which sprouting
from crannies and fissures of rocks
spreads a green veil over the roaring
or murmuring stream
in the tremendous chasm below.'

Freshness of tumbling waters
                    purity of mountain air.
An old temple marks the site of the source,
          a fine column of granite, a terrace —
And across the foam and roar of the waterfalls

               Look up
          to the cavern and   the top of the sublime
     precipices above

Seaward when the sun floods this profound gorge
     with golden light
          fantastic buttresses and rounded towers
               of this mountain rampart are revealed
And it is here

Adonis meets Aphrodite for the first
and the last time

And here his mangled body
is buried
And here every year his flower

the red anemone blooms
among the cedars of Lebanon

and his river runs red
to the sea
'fringing the winding shores
of the blue Mediterranean
whenever the wind sets   inshore
with a sinuous band of crimson'

Once a year his passing is a cause
for lamentation and commemoration
In March
      when early flowers
            bloom baskets
are filled with earth and planted
  with wheat
and flowers.   Tend the fast growing shoots

   for eight days these gardens of Adonis
      then flung into the sea
with his image
      as sacrifice
   to the new growth of the season

and with songs that the lost one
        will return
   and ascend to heaven
  and ascend into sprouting wheat
     into passionate   life again.

Tender life again.

SPRING 1992
WITH THANKS TO
SIR JAMES GEORGE FRAZER

July '92 at Naropa

With the term 'counter-poetics' we might ask

'counter' to what. With self   determination
you can do it in your basement.
Do   *something*

Allen Ginsberg has been busy   taking pictures

for the past 30 minutes
of Amiri Baraka
with the lens cap on his camera

'Texts tremble beyond the veil
Eruption of the marvelous
into everyday life'
— P.L. Wilson

Just where did these thoughts go?

Desperate to do something of charming

Creativity. Weed whip the hypericum.

Talk to Jack and Cass on the phone.

Ride bicycle out into the night.

JUNE 15, 1992

Midnight

Phone call from Cass
Jack wants us to sing
  Willow Weep For Me

What about Beyond the Blue Horizon
  Cass looks up the lyrics
  We sing it several times

The Little Slipper

You gave to me
  to encourage Phenomenology

FOR JACK CLARKE
JULY 9, 1992

Sunday Bay Lookout Check Up

A few party
boats looking for labor
day fish   Willow leaves still

Still have not started to fall
Reef barely shows
thin crested breakers
A dread cat meows behind
this back ego dissolve memory
Mental acrobatics song sparrow
song now here.   Same cast
of characters half a year later
going thru a season

Mild mannered
morning sun path glittering
directly into the path
of the writer.
Boy on bike arrives
with red jersey
Off on this bike

to look around
False Pacific Jingle
makes no sound

SEPTEMBER 6, 1992
8:30 AM

Passing through the Garden

Jim Anderson phones to tell me Max did not
respond to any of the life support systems
when they found him this morning. So he's gone.
   Max who always responded eloquently with memory
      to his mates who passed
on before him. A minute of this news, then adds
         Labor Day was such a success yesterday,
      the music! Max was there looking pale
   but distinguished with his drawing book, a new
drawing pad of perfectly etched sketches in pencil

He must have heard the saxophone of Clarence Clemons
      and all the hometown friends who play
     the music, play the jazz

  This early morning dream   I am coming thru the back
lot on the way to the house when I come across
a large wooden shrine, rectangular with a small
     memorial board   Chinese characters written
upon it, precise landscape.   I see a form

   passing through the garden
    and shout Out!   Stay out of the garden!
    and awake at the sound

This afternoon's walk around Duxbury Reef white shell
   sand pure beach observation thinking of Max,
cool, jaunty, stylish to his times.   *Millions*

   of sooty shearwaters flying north along the coast

a long single low line
        above the water as long
    as we can see
  for as long
  as we watch.
                Vast

TUESDAY, SEPTEMBER 8, 1992
FOR MAX CROSLEY

'No Escape'

'the desire to change
is fundamentally
a form of aggression towards yourself'
— *Pema Chodron*

NOVEMBER 9, 1992

Ava Gardner after Christmas

Cold air rushing under door

    Thunder, it's raining.   Reading *Ava, My Story*
left at porch door by Bill Berkson, neighbor.

'The truth is the only time I'm happy is when
I'm doing absolutely nothing.'

    A gust, a torrent, the sun.
    Better than H.D. writes Bill on title page.

Browsing; a semi-contented mind.

JANUARY 1993

If Bird Gets Noisy

Bird! Queen of the Night!
    (shake sarong in front of cage)

Bird! Queen of the Night!

    (if squawks continue
        put sarong over cage)

HOW JON QUIETS
HIS PARROT
FEBRUARY 4, 1993

Gliding steps   Gliding steps   We are at the edge

of the ocean & land   and a fire
is burning at the tip of the incoming

tide turns and carries the dried
petals you toss in the wind toss

in the flames and you are saying goodbye
goodbye so gracefully

ERNESTO AT AGATE BEACH
ON HIS WAY TO JAPAN
FEBRUARY 13, 1993

When Philip Whalen Had Heart Surgery

Dreaming, a lot of us are lying down together. Philip
is next to me. He is having trouble breathing
His breath is irregular
I breathe deeply, slow everything down
We get in synch together
The air is calm

I call him at the hospital the next morning
The voice says, You no speak Russian?
Is he putting me on?

A year ago when he was ill
        Philip thought he was on his way to Moscow

Very anxious I call him at home
     He answers, How're *you* doing, you ok?

MARCH 11, 1993

Again   recognizing
            the impediment of quirky sadness
Where does it come from? This shortness
            of teary breath — there!   it's gone
      in a sleepy time funneling of physical emotion.
It's not so bad.   What is it?
                              I hope Dave Haselwood
does not think too badly of my shortness of control
                  on the camping trip.   Can't you just
      let it go, those impediments. The anxiety
  of packing up 'things'.   We drove over a thousand miles
      on that seven day trip, circumambulated the Siskiyou
    Mountains, sacred to Karok, Yurok and Tolowa people.
But abrasiveness in the back of the truck where I lay seeing
    row upon patches of mountains, shaved of trees.
      And look around, where did the money, the wood
go.   Don't see it here, didn't stay for long.
          One immobile rabbit as guardian
      for the empty campground
                              Fallen fir giants
            rest around. Mossy rivulets abound
                  With great sorrow we left

            the beautiful place
    we *had* to leave   that beautiful place.

                              JULY 6, 1993

64

I am *not* going to be intimidated
by myself
Outflanked by, upstaged by
this former self of yesterday
which left a pretentious array
of books to read, sources to pull
the western mind into shape

SUNDAY AUGUST 8, 1993

I better go water
the lettuce
then I have to go listen to Zen tonight

MONDAY AUGUST 9, 1993

He   said
it took me 10 years of meditation
to discover I enjoy breathing
I can just   enjoy breathing

THURSDAY, AUGUST 12

Elliptical and irregular
              white cloud line
       around almost full
       moon tonight outside
  where teaching really   happens —
       I mean learning

SEPTEMBER 1993

Lay It to Rest Where You Are

After Agate Beach Reef
with remnants of   Jim Brodey's ash and bone
over hands   under nails

Watched the passage
            through shiny shale channel
of glitter dust and bone and rose tossed petals
moving along with the wavelets south

'You got to be thin
to get through the waves.   The waves
are coming . . . ' J.B.

Holding the last pink rose aloft
wind from the south holds it up.   'Let it go!'
shouts Berkson
      Western gull flies north.
Put it down   Where you are   I do

Return home   rinse hands with hose
            over compost heap
                  in our garden

SEPTEMBER 2, 1993
ASHES CEREMONY WITH
BILL BERKSON
BILL & DEBBY BECKMAN
AND BOB GRENIER

Full   of birds in the first
        soft rain of the year, gold and white crown
            sparrows, one rufus sided
                and three brown
            towhees, the energetically scratching fox
        sparrow, the ten members
    of the quail flock, the remaining song sparrow
whose mate   got ate by the black cat
            last week, anna hummingbird blur, red
        finch, the pair of red
    shafted flickers, and those noisy scrub
jays we always chase out
        of the garden by clapping our hands,
            the mockingbirds, the flock
    of robins in the pine looking at the bright
berries of the cotoneaster soon to make them drunk
kinglets, wrentits, they're all here now
            in this rain, in the gather dome

                                OCTOBER 1993
                                FOR JACK COLLOM

SUDDENLY!

The *same* Moon   in the next century!

February 27 Sunday

His eyes were rolled up into his head
and he was in deep distress
when they pulled him off the channel beach
yesterday and took him to the rescue center
to be force fed as he hadn't eaten for four days
after his mother abandoned him.   She was out
of her element being young with her first birth
which happened on the most public part
of the town's beach.
Around the clock watching went on until a week ago
when she took him further north up the beach a bit
for privacy which was not to be had.
Horses practicing jumps, dogs, dirt bikes, curious
humans.   She leaves him in the full moon lighted waters
This is too hard.

BABY ELEPHANT SEAL
BORN FEBRUARY 9, 1994
BRIGHTON BEACH

Daily meditations
make me so keen
I fall asleep
in the middle of the afternoon, quickly
dream into another world promptly forgot

The sun hot in the airless room
idle bird chatter
What's the matter with a consciousness doze
Hiding from the body mode
a plot unfolds unknown to the writer; the dreamer
is going beyond   behind the sunset   upstairs

MARCH 28, 1994

Don't want to do anything electronic
    Sky all streaked
   so tired
   of memory as content

If the machines do it do we have to read it?

Something is brewing in a windy
      grey laced sky. Churning
   over the flocks gathering
   up for departure.

Can the radio   do it, can the soup
   move it, blow us away
get my nephew out of his black depression?

Have you seen my yappy little yellow dog?
Well no.   The neighbor's doggy ate him.

APRIL 14, 1994

How *Does* one attain that popular narrative
tone so conducive to rendering the ancients
immediate and palpable?
Pretty intimate   thru illusory   time
and with a lurch of a heart   beat
his hand is on my shoulder
'Save all the good parts'
in a low and throbbing tone
'and the gossip'
the beauty light
in the late afternoon

CONVERSATION WITH
ALLEN GINSBERG
APRIL 1994

Bill Brown is too short of breath

to walk up the steps to his room
in the Blue Heron Inn.

What are you having for dinner tonight?
I've already taken care of it.
What did you have?
I'm too tired to talk about it.

I'm Bill Brown and I'm looking at a final spot.

APRIL 15, 1994

In our Yard
Brown Thrasher a very rare

visitor for the past 45 days got its
picture in the Hearsay   News
            under an ad for Madame Blavatsky
and left town the next day
        in the late May rain.

MAY 3, 1994

Town Hall Reading with Beat Poets

> 'The enlightened man is one
> with the law of causation'
> — *Mumon*

Ed Sanders onstage telephones William Burroughs
in Lawrence, Kansas, who stayed home 'because
my cats need me'.   I go hear him from the back
of the hall. Then it's near time for me to read.

Leaving I pick up some trash clogging the exit door.
It's my book, *Going On!*   What I'm reading from
tonight, those
    'understated Buddhist influenced miniatures'
      (says the next day's *NY Times* review
        of the event)

And it's *my* big dusty footprint on the cover.

MAY 19, 1994

/

It's different here now having been

to the other coast and returned to hit
the sharp edge of new linear lines and old old
     roar pouring over it

New/old   just habitat words of existence
Dick Gallup calls
Joe Brainard died three hours ago

A pair of mourning doves eating seeds
     at the table

Wednesday 6 PM
May 25, 1994

Compassion is

'the ability to react freely
and accurately in any situation,

the endless dimensions of this moment.'

— *Issan Dorsey*

May 31, 1994

Watching TV

Ahoy! Electronic nightmare . . .
      You don't see many Skunks watching TV
    that is, if you are watching the tube
   you never get to see Skunk outside strolling
  in the full moon towards the compost.   Good Evening.
He lifts his tail.   I'm just strolling,   so all is well
with the smell.

     A topographical enlightenment is swooning
in the back yard. Look at the sky tonight!   View
  the promenade of crisp hedges today.   'The world
    around us is workable' when the mind
  is unfettered and away from the tube, the screen;
the eyeball engaged in a back lighted room — mind tomb.

Then full moon Skunk appears   delightful
            with tiny frightful screams.

JUNE 23, 1994

It's lonely
on this road

Hitching down
to see Bill Brown
leave town

and he won't
be back
again
Oh no

Oh no

FRIDAY JUNE 24, 1994

80

On the Other Side

On the other side of the sliding glass door
    about six feet away —
               the scenic deer prunes the privet
    thoroughly.

Look at the black stripe around her muzzle
           her confident youthful grazing

in these small patches of scrub.   In olden times
        the voice of the deer
            'was deemed a poetic thing'
        with its 'sad satiety'
         Say what?   To the quiet muteness facing me —
    so quick to catch movement,
          self conscious with beauty and food
    frozen with regret
   too ignorant to move away
In the slanting sun setting, still 'imagining' the quiet
    muttering of contented doe feeding

Lost in old time haiku, 'three times it cried'
    and was heard no more
       Vanishes in the out of doors.

December 10, 1994

Terrace Roads slumps into the Canyon

Just one access to the Mesa now
      with a night stew of Emerson
    until midnight mist light drizzle
and water laden sky turns into downpour
     over pastures of ghosts
        and morning woods of angels.   Does a place

have its own Memory?   I'm on the river
    and cut off by the flood.   What is free
   from cause and effect?   The poetry song stone
that gives off overtones.   The quest
   is to find those lost vibrating overtones
 of the poetry stone.   Along the trail
of your little town, sheltered since your birth,
   the beautiful land.   Intense nostalgia
    invades my soul! Carrying Ita
all last night protecting
   that warm old cat body
    in my arms to get her to a place
  of respite, comfort, and safety.

God makes an impenetrable screen
     of pure sky, pulsating
   undulating, casual.

JANUARY 1995

82

I Blinked My Eyes, Looked Up
And Everyone Was 25 Years Older —

When you're alive you get to
    recognize hematite,
azurite, smoked quartz
     lovely eh?
        in sticky black silk

       And watch simplicity
            become complex in management
  'Only bow when bowed to'

      Go look at the sunset
Inspiration for a bunch of numbers
    heralding the close of the Xian calendar
      and new age metaphysical smoothies

Suddenly, I looked up, and everyone had white hair
People go in and out of your life, and your life
is a room filled with flowers and a kitchen cooking supper
and you have wrested the inscrutable from the obvious

or the other way around

We are called the exquisite bloom of February
We are called wild and grow freely

Very very annoying are people who arrive
an   hour and a half late for lunch.

                   MARCH 1995

"Replacement Buddhas"

The altar of Buddha is dark
The room has been taken
by the dolls.
— *Gyodai*

What do all those Buddhas *mean*
at the museum, brought from elsewhere?

Rhetorically, What do these apparitions signify?

"A magician mutters a spell over stones
and pieces of wood and produces the illusion"

of Buddhas and humans and animals and houses
"which although they do not exist in reality

seem to do so." And some people blinded
by this magical hokum-pokum

hanker after what they see — The Buddhas and fast
cars, race horses and glamorous people —

forgetting they are just stones & bones
pieces of wood

Translucent like last night's dream

FROM *The Life of Naropa*
MARCH 18, 1995

84

Is There Any Way I Can Do This Any Better?

No, this is fine.
        Quail calling.
   Perhaps on the psychophantic sidelines
there is an amusing sibilant whisper — 'Art!
    Poetry! Negligees!   NEA's!'
        Here they come with precision
walking and clucking.

You don't give a blank about quail anyway, do you.
What you want is some positive moolah, peer recognition
    in headlines.

Little black faced, little brown feathered people
You are about the right distance from the world —
wild, but dependent upon my attractions
to you as friends of the late afternoon.

A handful of poems for the year
    so far mind won't push open and extend beyond
        Oh America, Oh California, Oh Bolinas
        Give me your corny ears.

What stunning reprisal for the decent
        Mexican indigenous soul to have NAFTA compete
        with daily bread — imported corn
        from USA north.

What if we live with very very little
and that's the law.

Very very little.   Green grass shoots, seeds,
            an insect or two,   always water

What do you think about this so far
        along in time
            feeling the age proceed
and feed as we've done?

                                        FOR JACK SPICER
                                        MARCH 25, 1995

Two for Robin Blaser

"The poems tend to act as a sequence of energies
which run out when so much of a tale is told."
— R.B.

He is pruning the privet

of sickly sorrow   desolation
in loose pieces of air he goes clip clip clip
the green blooming branches fall — 'they're getting out
of hand'   delirious and adorable   what a switch
we perceive   multiple
identities   when you sing   so beautifully   the shifting
clouds   You are not alone is this world
not a lone   a parallel world of reflection
in a window keeps the fire burning
in the framed mandala, the red shafted flicker
sits on the back of the garden chair in the rain
the red robed monks downtown in the rain   a rainbow arises

simple country   practices   thunder
lightning, hail and rain   eight Douglas Iris
ribbon layers of attention

So   constant creation of 'self' is a tricky
mess   He is pruning the loquat, the olive
which look real enough in the damp late morning air

May 15, 1995

Oh Goody
This Afternoon We're Going to the Holy Forest

I want to find the place
  of the adored one, an entrance
into the presence of the first loved
    by the flowing waters
  that give us water at night.
Need sustenance to come back
    to the place, remember the swinging
intimacy?   It was there wasn't it?
    Wasn't that the place of the delightful
  original form — the loveliest garden and park
found at the center

          of this quiz.

First you declare your intention
Second you start on the path
Third you must *find* the path
Fourth you affirm the answer

        that this thought continues after a break
      and that you revisit this place for a moment

      of familiar recognition if not understanding
            and continue telling the story

      of content content   and form.

MAY 15, 1995
MONDAY AFTERNOON

Wake Up

Wake up this morning and gingerly open the door

to the heart.   What

does it feel   like   now that Franco is   gone.

Yesterday   Duncan knocks   and firmly   closes
the door   behind him   'Franco

es nada mas' Just got

his letter dated seven days ago   the words take on
sweet   final   meaning

'I love   to   work

in the   cool   mornings

and meadows   with   the   whole   Alpine   show

are   terrific'

Terrific.

In the   whole   of   space

In the   whole   of Clear   New   Space

for   you.

AUGUST 27, 1995

Floating of the Silver Chinese Paper

'Would you put this piece
of Chinese paper into the ocean
in honor of Franco'
            — *Louise Landes-Levi*

Wade into lagoon
        channel float paper
                with silver square

Moves out among
        these motes
                tear shaped
        notes of jumping
                sunlight on water

Rides on the surface glinting
        light a flat
                rectangle
Goes on   and out over
        the waves
                burnished yet bright

For many moments watch
        the movement into the main
        channel and out
                        into the waves
        of the final row
            before the open sea.
A dog swims by.

Blinking code and beacon light
Passes beyond the congregation
of flashing sun on water

And goes   away   out there

SUNDAY
OCTOBER 1, 1995

'Hi!   It's Tom'

No more phone calls ever again

NOVEMBER 14, 1995

Mythical many antlered white buck
under burned black tree
nibbling new green grass
Stop the car!

NOVEMBER 30, 1995
MT. VISION

The storm is upon us
Where is the wand of unawareness
Did I throw it out the door last night?

DECEMBER 1995

View North

Back dropped
    blue-grey clouds
        warm lull
    a spot of sun
in this clearing
        of moment transferred —
a perfectly peaceful point
    of view —

Larry Eigner's window.
    Salute you Larry!
        Seagull cries 3 times
    and then the crow,
    also a reef grazer,
slowest, easiest,
        then smooth layers exhale —
Don't let yourself get away
            from that conversational
        tone line of the reef emerging
        low tide, windless

FEBRUARY 2, 1996
IN MEMORY/LARRY EIGNER

95

Observe the lacy pink Coraline
Algae on the rocks at low tide

A stately form proceeds
over the centuries
one is at constant attention
Wake up

What's around you
is beautiful to the eye contented
in following the language of dream
when the habitat
became obtainable and many of us moved
in and fixed it up to make it liveable
in a most modest way, balancing drainage
and water
Thank you dream
for your confidence
in the avenues
of   'golden eternity'

'when the ephemeral is all that lasts'

With books the voice of the story over
and over again
Voice over again
Voice over

FOR LAWRENCE FERLINGHETTI
MARCH 1996

Bob Marley Night Saturday Downtown

Dreamlike   the lights have a dark smoky glow and the street
is filled with groups of people under twenty.   Car radios
groups of boys, groups of girls, three sheriff's cars.
Like spring break at Fort Lauderdale, but here everyone
goes home before morning.

At the Community Center the reggae is authentic, easy and
slow to dance to. The group, from Mendocino, has served
'jerked' chicken for dinner.   I go around back to see if any
barbecues are still set up.   The plaza is filled with vans,
their own encampment.

I walk up and start a conversation with a man and woman
cooking.   Like, Lovely evening, how lucky you can park in our
plaza, which we don't usually allow,   don't you love our
Community Center, and that's our freebox over there, etc.
She says, o God

they told me   there would be people like you   here.

MARCH 18, 1996

97

Why Did She Ask Us to Write This Way Anyway
the Mood Moves

Why do we even practice this craft while the radio is on
with Alastair Cooke's measured tones on the anti terror bill
in the early morning mesa moody overcast before the Dharma
Queen enters her Monday cleaning blues with vacuum cleaner
perusing the nothingness bound to get sucked into the bag
of the morning universe all over the world.   People I think
of you as one in this dreamy schwarm called earth and time
looking out in binocular vision as the Pandas climb into
an increasingly smaller giant bamboo forest to only remain
as stuffed bears the kiddies take to bed.   Fight for the right
not to be born HUMAN this time around
                                        and come out as hungry baby
tiger ready to devour the endless tumbling Boddhisattva
Prince who's given up his ghost for tiger doggy bag.   Yummy
is the human who enters the food chain as food for mammal
equals like Grizzly Bear who has to stop at the border for
hikers.   Generous is the gift of well fed human flesh to
Maestro White Shark cruising among the beings of the ocean.

The animals should eat back!
                    Homage to Kerouac

APRIL 22, 1996

I Need Some Tea to Wake to Beautiful

clear warm evening on the way to Alice's reading
           'The Descent of Alette'.   We are in

a new world, lilting, in the caves, a narrative
        flow in tune, her voice twined round any overload
             of world stuff.   The buzz words make
                 running in circles crazy like quail
        trying to mate   Where ARE you   Where ARE you

   Living and dying   just par for the course
       What did we do to deserve *this*?

   Dark blue Lupine   Very white Douglas Iris
          Singularly orange California Poppy   Jumping
on the band wagon of April on the coast   Ant
in front of Ocean   is very quiet

              'Our Abbot' is one in the family
   of poets who kisses this hand, adieu.   Reflects all this
            polishing & cleaning, sitting down and parting
         that poor tattered veil of being
      both dead and alive in time
   as a perfect gift

MAY 1, 1996
FOR ALICE NOTLEY
& PHILIP WHALEN

So,　well,　now,　You've got it
                    Alone
            behind the scenes with the dishes
                and a fast embrace
        with Robert Duncan's *Hestia.*
                — I practiced being true
                to you and desperately
Angry also just for the force
        of that energy as independence
    and the foresight that nothing
                lasts forever

        — PUSH OUT　　THE BREATH LINE —

    Please no more ad nauseam dinky words
    down left hand margin of paper
    datedly practiced by second generation
    New York School　stuck on their typewriters

                                SEPTEMBER 1996

100

Phone Call from Milosz

"American poetry equals an enormous collection
of snapshots from which we divine the things observed
and the mind of the observer."

"Allen Ginsberg's *Howl* was a leap, but only owing
to its somewhat hysterical American apocalypse and rage."

Are you going to interrupt me in my coastal snooze?

What are you going to do?   Read all day long?

Crazy fox sparrow scratching back and forth
back and forth, back and forth

And that's the end   of the day again

SEPTEMBER 1996

Poison Oak for Allen

Here I am reading about your trip to India again,
with Gary Snyder and Peter Orlovsky. Period.
Who took cover picture of you three

with smart Himalayan mountain backdrop
The bear?

SEPTEMBER 2, 1996

Saturday Night Chicken

You are empty at this moment
just a nanosecond
after second wind

And thoughts of Joe Dunn ill
in Newburyport
Imagine a moon dust walk

And a new sadness at loss
introduced which feels more raw

Deep sighs and spontaneous good will

'Revenge is a dish
best served cold.'   Just take it!

Your lot

Be content with your lot

Green lavender, clothing of seaweed
minuscule pieces of jade

Being content with this lot is your life
It's a lot

More than enough

SEPTEMBER 7, 1996

Looks like it's going to rain any minute

It's been four months since my mother died, aged 92
    and emotions are smoother now.   Not the depth
    of the details of taking care
    of her earthly remains.   'Rest upon the Beautiful Shore'
    becomes her reminder in the softness of Santa Barbara
    sunshine and weather.

Her house was sold.   Left one closet full of wooden coat
            hangers the other with pastel plastic hangers
            separated according to color.

November 16, 1996 9:16 AM

Sunday it rained all night

I dreamed Liz Tuomi got married all of a sudden
She has a bright radiant smile.

There is a November winter wetness steady ocean rumble
I just ran into a rat in the shed
An involuntary horrible scream

The quail calling are landing over the fence
The fence is new, about 10 years ago

What do you expect from an 'I' this morning?

NOVEMBER 17, 1996 8:50 AM

Snapshot for Lew Welch   25 Years Later

Hold on to the bright

Time memories   Bolinas Bay
eases in   with flat
smooth curves

in front of the slope which gradually
falls away through the years

A turkey buzzard
family of three are hunched
atop a bent-over branch.   One
raises its wings to the early
morning sun to dry

Directly down-slope behind them
white lacy patterns
of water fill the picture

A while to groom   and wake
to small circles breaking
the surface of the bay down there —
a sure indication
of edible water dwellers

seven surfers cruise the mouth
of the lagoon

Curving antlers of a young
buck rise through the scrub
at the bottom of the gully

A bit of transplanted
pampas grass waves airily

The turkey buzzard
with wings outstretched is still

a totem. The deer still
as it gazes frozen up-slope
at me penning this down
for you.   Then

such a beautiful exiting
white furry rump

9:11 AM
OVERLOOK CLIFF EDGE
SATURDAY
OCTOBER 19, 1996

No use creeping thru the fog with a driver who won't

Attempting meditation this morning mind jumps all
        over the place give up go into
           brain the truth goes on so what

The sky gradually lightens up and darkens again. Anselm's
"A joint in time in the great carpentry"
   reminds me of   Jim Gustafson's crazy speed induced trip
    here when he bought a house on the expensive little mesa
but of course he doesn't have any money
      at all I had to tell the real estate
        broker when she tried to call his banker
          and the number didn't exist
            but he had a lot of shopping bags
             from the St. Francis
Hotel and stationery too.
          In earlier halcyon days we bounced a green tennis
ball back and forth three miles to town   bye-bye

                        NOVEMBER 20, 1996 9:10 AM

Dear dear little wrentit with white circle around your eye
    bouncing thru   red berries of   wild honeysuckle
    grey overcast and foggy   damp in the studio
the neighbor keeps his woodchipper going at a dull
    sickening roar hour after hour.   I do not wish
      him well, pulverizing his Mexican oak mulch.
Try to be *vast* now.   Remember this strand
       of conscious thinking vibrating like a watery
    jewel on the morning's cobweb.   All show, plunk
  it falls, so temporal, this attempt to cliché the moment.
As all falls silent.

DECEMBER 1, 1996

The gale was upon us in a second.   Was it the dope
brownies that made us feel so wet all
of a sudden the space between rain
drops was filled with rain.
This is a serious business
this existence thing
this life

without an umbrella and only
a black hat between thoughts
and the elements thundering
down in an obligatory
engulfing swoosh

DECEMBER 22, 1996

Bob Grenier old friend
lost him somewhere out there

at RCA Beach with his notebook and hand
style   I can't keep track

of his hours, anymore, they're all set
    up or getting upset
but no mistake, he's still

in the service of the muse hour

by hour
a chuckling serious inner

ear

tenaciously receiving
the messages

willing to skew those letters
        across a rock

    hard impudent and thrifty

DECEMBER 24, 1996

The storms of the season make me loose my reason

I NEVER have been able to spell 'lose' correctly —
Is it loose or lose?
And how can I remember to
spell right?   A rule or rhyme
in time would be divine —

Loosing the drainage causes puddling
    This is piddling rumination   I am sixty   And a black
cat looks at me from January 1997   run after it

    waving arms,   hissing   Get out!
        bird killer!   Bird habitat of the mesa
        gets smaller every year
        as vegetative imports move in
Who wants to eat datura or broom seeds or rely on free
    handouts   Who wants to know how to spell 'rely' really

right   I do   I want to be relevant, and interior also.
Revelations of insight, story   Where black cat comes
from, the household hearth, stalking the understory as
killer. The quick intermediary of lovers, it's ok if he's in
my bedroom.   A legendary priapus; but neither 'here' nor
'there' but in the space between, flowing along, quite nicely
thank you in retrospect.   However, in the moment often an
angry battle of dissatisfaction when the rains start falling
again.

    2 PM: Try not to provoke a reaction — go with the
pattern of energy, restore the original state of openness,
see how creative you feel, says Trungpa.   Making some

space again between 'this and that' for passion defeats its
own person in grasping instead of binding.
                                In a high springtime
            meadow plateau strewn with wild flowers and frisky
                        young mountain sheep

        I refuse to rewrite this,   but I did

                                            THURSDAY
                                            JANUARY 2, 1997

Returning Home

Great to be back to beauty
    green and clean where in memory
  this place reflected the doldrums of winter
holiday and death of the year,   restricted heart no coming
    thru the digs of necessity, all dignity gone
        in supplication to the face on the bar room floor,
        I cringe before thee.

What do you think?   Is this enough
    to get started on welcome back and ahead
  of the revolving wild lone — well not so wild not so
    lone when the story gets going.   Hang on

MARCH 6, 1997

You?

Was that you whistling for me, the snake in the shower?
The water doesn't really, in the long run belong
to any 'one'. The wild man on stage shouting the Prajna
Paramita.   'Poetry is about continuing Poetry.'   Look look
    look quickly

MONDAY
MARCH 10, 1997

115

An Apple, An Orange, and a Flashlight
Full Moon Eclipse with Comet

Glowing full in eastern sky
    just above the coast range
  grows slowly dark
from the bottom up

    Let us continually view
    the phenomena from the front
porch chair with binoculars
  recalling our ancient awe
    that the gods are swallowing
our moonlight

    Viewed through bamboo
  hazy bands of black and silver
float across this handsome face

    And now higher in the sky
a clear bite devoured
    directly opposite the comet's
  smooth and silky tail

A final ghostly marble in relief

SUNDAY, 6:58 PM
MARCH 24, 1997

116

Wide Mind

Occupies a wide mind, a wide consciousness,
   front page, editorial page
The winds of spring are cold and keen from the sea
    Can one bring dead people to dinner?
      Constantly opening up those dark arms
      'I'm having a ball
          sleeping with my skeleton'   Allen
        before he dies

A harsh hawk-like call from the cypress hedge entrance
    come out   come out!   I am   I am   never
      been here before   See me? Stellar Stellar

Jay jaunty blue black

'Do you suppose it's him?'
'I was thinking the same thing.'

Day after A.G.'s passing
Sunday
April 6, 1997

117

Constantly Opening Up Those Dark Arms

'The love you have is the love you get'
— last words of Allen to Rick
on the phone 2 days before he dies

Belonged to everyone who read his poems, listened
    to his long breath tones
                Another long sigh
        of yet another memorial
    to bridge to the city

The White Crowns have already left, the Gold Crowns
    congregate daily, a handful of six, hanging out
      with the now pairing off quail

And there's a rapid banging at the door on a dark and lonely
   night 9:30 PM   'Don't you want to save
                     the Headwaters' Forest?'

    Do you realize we have NO protection
    between our living room couch and the front door?

      'What do you want?'
      'I want to discuss this with you.'
      'What! do you think I'm a nitwit, I don't know
        what's going on?'

        I resent door solicitations
        I'm busy watching a rerun of *Blow Up* on TV

Philip says on the phone, they all like that Tibetan stuff
    better than Zen, the flash, the tulkus, the reincarnation
Nobody showed up at the zendo this morning, Philip
        practically blind, fumbling around, lighting candles,
        burning thumb on incense   Ouch!

    bang shin on Buddha.

We will not settle for anything less!

    And then it's brown towhee tsk-tsk-tsk-tsk
            announcing dawn like a cricket alarm clock
    — small favors of intimacy at home

                                    April 19, 1997

                                    119

I find it difficult to utter a meaningful utterance but

I *can* take the lightweight branch of a tree from a window
five stories up and let it propel me gently to the ground —

a combination of flying and floating, reminding myself
not to hurry the process into a crash landing.   I can also
stay out from under the feet of an elephant on a narrow
bridge — but this requires some assistance and a tip
to the owner.

I also believe gardens should be planted with native seeds.
But to recommend an overview of how to sustain a floating
immigrant population like our own, I am at a loss.   Of
course I believe one should be entertained by the imagination
and am against disgusting profit, but what about hoarding
ideas and feelings.

                              And the neighbors who park
their car on your property, which you now want to landscape
with shrubs. But we've parked here for 10 years. Are you
telling us we *can't* do it now, this is a TRADITIONAL USE!

Well, you would like to point out,   why don't you cut
back a little bit of your non-native bottle brush and put
your 'traditional' parking there, and then you could have
your traditional parking on your OWN traditional
land . . . . PLENTY of room there.

APRIL 29, 1997

Arthur Okamura's Pipul Tree's Bodhi Leaf

All these sentient questions
   for Ficus Religiosus Indica's dark green shining
      leaf and long drawn tapering tip, trembles and shimmers

with just a suggestion of breath, awareness of air, change
     and motion   before the human seated below
       in dark and desperate meditation becomes quote
         'Enlightened.'   The tree, a companion in mutual

awareness, a companion in mutual enlightenment,
   equally rooted in being   in one place
     in a meditative state with inalienable rights
       — 'all things' being interdependent and equal

A *tree* achieves 'Buddhahood'
        2500 years ago reflected now in this ancestor
         leaf compiled of the most complex
           ingredients of creation: Sun
            Cloud and Water,
                Earth, Time, Space, Mind, Universe . . .

      Like any leaf
         from every tree.

MAY 1997

ARTHUR'S LEAF DESIGNED FOR POETRY FLASH'S
WATERSHED ENVIRONMENTAL POETRY FESTIVAL,
GOLDEN GATE PARK BANDSHELL, MAY 17, 1997

First Nation

Back in   First Nation time, morning of the world time
the sun has yet to arrive, keeping all in a silver keening.

Attack a chore and stay there
          Imports are tossed
                    on the compost.   This
                        is about weeding the unwanted
                        and uninvited

plant life out of the ground.
                    A very short stop for roots to stay.
                    It's labor

intensive and not mine, cruising the Sunday paper
filling an empty mind with instantly forgettable
facts of global life.   Hello

did you sleep
well in the New World Swing?

            By the Round House they go inside young men
            with suitcases and punk clothes. Gather their power

            keeping the door closed
      Come out birds, deer
flicker feather headbands, turkey feather tails,

shiny abalone buttons.   Way-ah
it's always been.

SUNDAY JULY 20, 1997
AFTER 'BIG TIME'
AT KULE LOKLO, PT. REYES

(Hushed tone of voice)
    Does Air have Memory?

The crickets are telling
this story tonight

                          JUNE 1997

124

A violin plays a sprightly 10 note theme

Practicing footwork for the tennis court
    are you a man or woman? You must have your
       identifying earring. Pablo Neruda
          I love his poetry says an earnest and handsome
         dark haired Italian tennis player

Abduction in the city, turn the corner, and she's gone.
I love his poetry too, did you see the movie?

My idea was that there would be these sudden images
from the dream, and the violin theme so sweetly played

with space between, no need to make a narrative or
tonal bridge.

That clump of bamboo is *dead*, diseased.

And then send it off to someone, who's appreciative
if not puzzled.

AUGUST 25, 1997

125

Everyone is Flying Very Well, Easily in the Sky
Kitty, Popped Out a Like a Cork,
Soars Round and Round in the Dark Starlit Sky

One would just like to fly out in pure invention
and freshness. Wisdom too.

The mythic overtones of a dome
that is not exactly BE HERE NOW which she has practiced so
long she hasn't any retention or memory. Just here. Now.
Duh.   Well, not really that bad, because the instant dream
transport tries to feed her information.   Did it happen in
some psychic manner or had she just got too stoned
with her friends.
Whatever the serendipitous interventions are
they make her feel the universe around is full of mysterious
reverberations.
Is it creative non-fiction,
literary journalism, or factual writing with a flair. A few
short lines every day on the weather.   It was high tide
and there wasn't any beach left.   How could they get there

to clean it up?   When the tide came in, the fog dropped
privately around the groomed and ungroomed grounds.   A deer
bitten sunflower produced a small bloom. A thank you card in
the mail tells her poems look fine in the magazine, signed
Pete.   Who is Pete.   What magazine.

On equinox morning the first
gold crown sparrow of the season arrives, such a gift
of timing.   Then 50 quail, a swarming brown feathered mass.

The huge tree rat   is caught in a large trap.
So sad.   It stashed little nibbled apples.
It didn't know it was a *bad* rat.

They want to destroy this tall tower
which is part of the church but the native people cling to
its sides. They save it. It settles into place. They are
Indio, and deeply religious.   I go into the church with them.

I am with 'Asians' on a nighttime picnic paddling down a small
river near the ocean.

Time for robins to eat the ripe berries of the cotoneaster
        and get gah-gah.
                        Rufus sided towhees come back
to the same spot under the coffee-berry trees
   to scratch and eat every year
                See the seasonal return is confident

   of itself. Confides itself in repetition
        never quite the same.

SEPTEMBER 24, 1997

I thought, I'll make it *so* simple

anyone can get it   understand
                not that it would be beautiful
        or anything like that.   Remote   maybe baby talk.

So lost that taut story, the reason to head through
        classic epics to have structure for understanding
        however   'Western'.

Then with the assumption of Pacific   characters
        became mammals or birds, frogs.

An attitude of listening repose   drifting
        through a cumbia tea-dance with Rhamus Californica

        a bushy partner
    and an up-beat early evening towhee

        who's not so wild anymore

OCTOBER 25, 1997

Grateful

After two months in Mexico

and continual rain storms here
      to find this studio

not slurped away by a subpocket
of suction hell.   Anyway

notebooks a bit damp
and mold has taken
      the last of the faded blue atticus

butterfly.   Still *dry*   framed
pictured of pensive youngster —

'Nobody loves me
 I'm going into the garden
 to eat worms.'

And looking fairly immaculate —

    Trungpa's 'First thought
         Best thought'
      which makes it seem   easy

    'Yesterday I ate two smooth ones
    And one woolly one.'

FEBRUARY 11, 1998

Bring Your Jungle Along

Full of sledgehammers and compassion —
of which the latter is exactly what?

Bleeding heart liberal do-gooder
bullshit come
passion

(which at least produces outrage
before exhaustion sets in)

Or working through the words of 'forgiveness'
or whatever the blank you want to call it

Like 'I know our ancestors once belonged
to countries that tried to wipe each other out *entirely*'
spoils of war and subjugate etc. But forget it!
Forgive.   It's all in the past.

It's this minute that's important
between you and me, and of course
the future of this minute

and how its course is already set, that minute
behind us called history.   And of course we read

so we remember.   And how *were* you to know.

FEBRUARY 23, 1998 5 PM
FOR KEVIN

Stupidly Inspired

It's true

the cricket ate the lace curtain in the studio,   not
relegating itself merely to the hearth, escorted

out the door rapidly in a teacup.   There.   You'll like it
better in the wild world of woodchips and ferns.

                    Bad Vibes a mere drape
for the deeper expositions of life and words. Something
meaningful about existence,   awareness of enlightenment
in a lifetime.   Get it while you're alive, can't find it

when you're dead. The simple timeless 'it's all right' satori
no no, that's right,   you got it right,   believe it.

MARCH 21, 1998

131

Sunday's Graces

are at war, swimming down a river,
espionage, nightclubs, filmy dresses, cigarettes,

tax collectors, lazy piano jazz.   It's 8:36 AM
and the Graces are active

they won't sit still

MAY 26, 1998

Well, you know
        I love what I've found

    here   next to a precise tidal zone

Finally one falls over the edge. Onto the shore line.
The Librarian says he was cheerful, but *too* cheerful
            if you know what I mean.

                              JUNE 12, 1998

Throw Away Mind

What's the use etc.   Do they have classes
on how to die? I wondered last
week, a hard earned grade or proficiency degree
in writing Living Trusts but
            just last night the baby quail appear

    in dream, tentatively showing
      themselves for the first time sleeping
    upstairs still looking
for a diagnosis for joy, for the first fresh
    steps

JULY 22, 1998

The dew sweet law
   is not flowing
      literature
         but is still

Open morning
   after morning
      and totally excellent

As the bachelor quail looks up
   in the quiet air

   all the food is his

JULY 23, 1998
READING ABOUT
NAGARJUNA

'Send some kind of sign at least'

'Nothing matters. You do not matter. You are not
   worth telling the truth to. Your most deeply
      held belief, your most pressing need
        is nothing.'
           Do you feel an insane rage, a desperate
falling away?

Welcome back to your life, she says.
   I see a new flicker

        feather lying on the front
porch like a calling card. Matching the two
   placed with the bell on the door.
      My heart
pounds. Can life
   be so good, am I recognized?

JULY 24, 1998

For the Pittasporum Tenuifolium Outside
the Studio Window

Much too hard to understand all
these words about words
beyond words

'respectful, considerate, sympathetic'

Alas poor seedling you have gotten
out of hand, too tall, now
you are almost a tree
and must be 'removed'

A pampered euphemism for 'killed'
for you take away my sun
you are out of place, you were careless

Your seed volunteered itself.   Goodbye.

We both become 'liberated', unattached
to your form
and become congenial

if not congratulatory
at our mutual trembling
in the attentive noon breeze

SUNDAY, JULY 26, 1998

137

Landscape Rising

These people may not be everybody's cup of tea
      but they are each other's cup of tea

They live, and have always lived, in Cookham
      near London   where the census

of swans takes place.   Christ in a pastel

landscape floats into a town, looking like Cookham
      but called Jerusalem
And in the wilderness Christ rises from sleep

his robes rising too like a white morning glory
from a ditch his arms pointed above his head

Portraits of his second wife in their unconsummated
marriage show her naked on a bed
                  an untempting piece of meat

While outside the edifice holding this history
      of the piercing-eyed painter is a spot

where Frances Willard in 1883 stood and said
'We are one world of tempted humanity'

becoming the first world organizer of women
      on what is now a golf course of mediocre players

directly on the bluff looking towards the headlands
of Marin County and the Golden Gate Bridge

STANLEY SPENCER'S
PAINTING EXHIBITION
AT THE LEGION OF HONOR
AUGUST 21, 1998

Some Choice

'With Joanne it's the fact that she has chosen to live
in this little town and not be famous

and to perform her life in this highly spiritual but not
draggy way, this really interesting and colloquial way
in the woods'

— FROM A DISCUSSION
BETWEEN X & Y
Gare du Nord VOL. I, #3
1998

Living a Spiritual Life in the 'Woods'
for Alice and Douglas

At least it's simple
           to mind the wild
           honeysuckle and now the monarch

    butterfly has returned
for the season's changing

light deepens

October 2

    Now you see
      her now
    the woods for the trees
    and light morning breeze
    and a car trundles
down the dirt road but it is not

for her the noon whistle blows
announcing the end

    of the morning sitting
cross legged with cross thoughts

October 3

141

Life is short and

there is no
one to talk

to on
the telephone

OCTOBER 4 SUNDAY

empty white rocker in empty white room

OCTOBER 5

Anna's humming bird

does its familiar dart around
the corner of the house but its food
the red fuchsia
has just gone   has just gone to the dump

OCTOBER 6

142

'We must uncenter our minds from ourselves'
— *Robinson Jeffers*

'. . . overcome your fear of goo
Come and taste the good goo stew'
— *Gerrit Lansing*

Absolute first sighting of Grey Squirrel on Mesa
Descending nose down tall eucalyptus

It's Allen Ginsberg's medicine-tree squirrel
followed me here from Boulder's Naropa campus

Here to eat the neighbor's introduced Mexican oak
acorns from Chamula in Chiapas
where they boycotted the vote
in recent election defying the ruling PRI
party which holds power by deception
repression & fraud.

OCTOBER 6   5PM

143

Calm & Cool Economics

I'm the World Economy

and I don't WANT

To be Stimulated

October 7

Did I Call You?

Was it you   I called up
Last night?

October 8, 1998

144

It's So

It's so hot and sleepy at two this afternoon
    and sad too like a skeleton bracing itself
        Do you think some stray word

Will electrify this mess or does one just
    give in to the empty space of the afternoon
        O go to the beach drag yourself to the shore

OCTOBER 20, 1998

Shark knife and the soft night is gone

The raccoons last night sounded
    like enraged hippos
      objects knocked

      about in the wind, big branches
    of the flowering

        purple flowering
          tree dahlia have broken

off to keep a narrow
unimpeded line

for the reader

is so undemanding
        Slip out thru that window
  as the storm squalls
      move over the Mesa

and see the lights come on again

D<small>ECEMBER</small> 1, 1998

What Is Unusual in This Cold Freshness of Hanging

the light lavender sharpness of cloth
on the clothesline is seeing

Fences   making   land into 'yards' when years ago
the living flowed   easily across paths of scrub
and trails to the ocean now gullies of poison
oak and slumping land

The leaves are gone from the willows, apples and plum
truly a winter scene   with gardeners
the neighbor employs daily speaking Spanish I can't
'get' but it's a job

no one else can or will do for the pay he gives
stability and enjoys his role of 'jefe'
too I suppose this is what living a long time
in one place adds up to comparisons and memories
not always for the better.

Like hearing over and over   the vicarious details
of sexual impeachment.   Of *course* I didn't do it,
I'm not going to kiss and tell   are you crazy?

DECEMBER 11, 1998

'Be it ever so humble'

Dappled big leaf maple light

                              reflected up
               from Papermill Creek runs
                  down Sir Francis Drake
          Boulevard of my dreams about British
          royalty although Kitty Kelley's is
       waste of time except to remind me Queen
     Mother's name is Elizabeth   and still
     alive. This association thru language *is* poetry
   to many   who like to slice it nice

          'The pathways are static
          mobility is dynamic
          and enlightenment is creative'
                    — *Naropa*

                              DECEMBER 15, 1998

Neurological pathways very rapidly sensitively moving over the body like 'feathers on a bird'

The mystic heat is tuned up in Naropa's awareness
Eternal delight, smoky, glittering, glowing, light

Sun rays, moon rays, lightning
rainbow space all fuse together

Authentic wealth, perfect life and beauty
Walk, sit, and fly in mid air.

Pretty great, eh. Do you realize these states
are described in a *book*?

A slippery attachment
to yearn after
ten thousand years old

on a crisp afternoon when bombs fall
a continent away

DECEMBER 19, 1998

Whilst the Impeachment Proceeds Guzzle Red Wine

And the dear companion climbs the tree
and cuts it down
and chops it up

            The quail are so cautious
       now the adolescent hawk is after them

they won't feed on the open grass
for the equinox

DECEMBER 21, 1998

Solstice

Just living in the dark time night time
day time flurry of white flakes across Bolinas
Bay green land of Tamalpais behind this Hiroshige
apparition of excitement high beauty familiarity

She falls to her knees shrieking It's
Snowing!

The nation is hurtling towards censure
of the wagging finger having probed and moved

onto the back of time   waving

DECEMBER 22, 1998

Can't We Rest Another Day?

Keep the fire
banked
and lively
with natural light
and pastel lilies
rose pink protea
silver candles
soft cheeses
fino sherry
numb heel
her dependence
on language
linguistic
veils   adoring her finery, she barely
walks relies on palanquins, transparent
overlays   circulation   bare

territorial jealousy   heart
of loneliness pared down
to a Townsend's warbler
catching the small gnats
along the cypress hedge
to maintain its high
pitched metabolism

Or in Robert Pinsky's words
sound (open mouth wide   say   ow!)
is the medium of the poet coming thru body

of said poet, 'the column of air inside the chest
shaped into sounds in the larynx and mouth'

   'the way words shiver and rumble and pass
     through the lips'

      hardly an epiphany

       but what do you expect when the dark
     fog rolls in and the quail trail through
with their characteristic rustle and clucking
  on the land outside your window
    at the end of the year

                    DECEMBER 27, 1998 6:12 PM

Naropa approaches his teacher
Instruction time again

How's it going boss?

Tilopa says   Come over here
and presses a burning stick into his flesh.   Yikes
this hurts!

Don't you remember this from before?

No limits to the knowable and the merriment
of the Gods and Goddesses over the ignorant
rebirth of the wayward human
which in the long run is really really painful

Here, I'll kiss it and make it better.

JANUARY 18, 1999

Try

very hard.   See
it wasn't so hard
but soft and warm to chase
the dream get worn out
give up again hold this vision
into a heavenly shield
against fear a 'wondrous
creativity'
against the bewildered
daytime   mind find
teachings in many realms.

APRIL 12, 1999

A Brisk Wind is Blowing
Thoughts to Philip on the Phone

The New York Times says I'm a Language Poet
Are you?
Of course not

Are you a Beat Poet?
No, I'm my own Poet

George Stanley says you're an Oregon Poet
Ha ha

Do you understand what deconstruction is?
No
Well if you don't, I won't keep trying

MAY 14, 1999

A Gift from Rick
Morning Dream June 14, 1999

Rick Fields and I
are on a peyote walk carrying flags

We are standard bearers
He has a large flag
I have a smaller one

But they have a somewhat Christian
insignia on them

Don't worry says Rick
Christ is a coyote

Open Amaryllis Salmon Pink & White

A Varied Thrush arrives

'Our friend Rick
is thinking of leaving us'

Gone
now really miss you

Only we know where
the daffodils are
buried underground

JUNE 1999

Today's got the bright

      cool awareness of fall and be careful
     you don't startle the quail on the way
    to write this   from an alarming
   squeaky chair that makes the baby
     robin respond in song

There they are!
    all along here
   one massive school
of anchovies

Their eyes shine
   don't they

As several thousand
pelican   and gulls
  mill about on a further
sandbar in the lagoon

  Meanwhile
    behind me on the little
town beach sit all
    nine town drunks
  drinking

This poem is more
like a picture
postcard   isn't it

romantic?   I'm in
god's fussy hands

leaving these words for you

SEPTEMBER 1, 1999
1:48 TO 4:08 PM
FOR JOHN WIENERS

160

We Are All Twenty-three, 1957

We're all 23, 1957. The Lantz dresses
  the red Capezios with silver buckles reheeled every week
    worn out from running up & down Grant Avenue on night
    adventures

    John Wieners staying sometimes at the apartment
      on Columbus   Hearing him at night in the kitchen
        with someone   I'm in the bedroom   he's always
          making toast I shout   leave the bread alone!
            he's with a Boston Junkie   What's she saying?
            She's an innocent, she really means the bread

Ah Phooey

Grafted apples for an entry.   Empty
  go through one set of rooms
    after another to get to the exit
     of conjugal living

Dragonflies diving south in brilliant orange
& red.   It all adds up
to a mindless equation of 'life' vs 'non-life'
and the essay on Eco-Poetics which according
to the editors 'needs a lot of work'
Phooey.   Real notes
    alive   an audible projection

It's a quiet night.   Then the crickets start talking
back and forth in their particular rhythmic tone
varying   with your thoughts.
                    Soon too frog chorus
with several voices.   The air fills
  with this chanting pulse talk   back and forth
    drifting. Vast. Kerouac bound.
    By merely listening,   you add your sound

NOVEMBER 15, 1999

162

Question to Anne Waldman after being interviewed by Bill
Berkson at The New College like they were at Club 21
sitting at a ringside table on November 19, 1999

"Do you think they should show on public tv a camera shot of
the inside of a Panda Bear's vagina getting artificial
insemination at an army base in Texas?"

Kathleen Fraser e-mails Anne the next day to find out if
Joanne Kyger is 'ok'.

It's so quiet
you can hear
the wasps sipping water
in the courtyard fountain

JANUARY 25, 2000
PATZCUARO

Return to that familiar
damp smell at dawn

Sparrows eat the plum blossoms

Old Dead Head
of sunflower still
stands propped
up in head high Kale
the Quail love to eat
so much

FEBRUARY 9, 2000

Recently

Recently, this life of mine, likes to stay 'home' more
comfortable in the dwelling and less

outside without a roof. Where rain or shine bones
should go everyday
                    thru the surrounding
               territory with the right shoes.

The jonquils, the daffodils, the narcissus, pale
and dark yellow faces loom thru the fog of a rainy day

Opening flashes to an underworld of historical familiarity
in an uncontrollable flight towards awakening

down under where memory is myth
and furnished with raw understanding of basic plots

Persephone is flashing towards her mother
'I'm coming back to the sun'

       — joy at recovering the lost one
             beginnings of a new crop, organic
                one hundred percent pure

SUNDAY, MARCH 5, 2000

166

Not Really April

Ever see robins sumo wrestle?

Robert Duncan is carrying on at a great rate
    in this almost empty room
        along with Jack Spicer, and Philip Whalen

and me who has wakened in the night
    to read the biography of Arthur Conan Doyle —
        practices spiritualism and goes to seances.

— the tattered lace curtain
        the severely pruned plum tree

        See this diagram? There's some truth
    in it you   on your narrow bed
    will appreciate,

    wildly patterned clothes to be returned
        to their owner. It's all a confusing
           sleight of hand with apologies accepted
               I think about you all the time but I still don't

know how to call you up

SUNDAY, MARCH 26, 2000

Post Consciousness

Implausible thoughts around very real spring flowers
    makes a perfection of digression
        as   the 'mind' goes out thru the eyes
        and wanders among objects —

      You are a purple tulip opening so wide
      your petals fall off

Now move those awful blue glass bunnies

APRIL 21, 2000

'Retirement'

An unfamiliar warble   9 times more

    cautious and deliberate   a public sound
in today's chapter of life
       and nameless unless I run for the binoculars
       and bird book
          which I cannot because I am busy

positing thoughts in this or that direction

    'against a cage of space' and reading
       The New Yorker, utmost voyeurism
        from a semi country life of retirement

    Whoa
       what a toss up
          for expanded consciousness
            that refuses to garden

   very much but loves to fuss
and prune with the mythology
       of under and   over tones

MAY 3, 2000

Your Heart Is Fine

Your heart is fine   feeling the widest
possible empathy for the day and its inhabitants

Thanks for looking at the wind
in the top of the eucalyptus
dancing like someone you know
well   ' I'm here   I'm here   I'm here!'

The wind picks up
a rush of leaves waving

wildly for your understanding
—apple, plum, bamboo
rooted and flourishing
next to your home
in the air   awake

without defect

JUNE 17, 2000

170

Sunday 26 November 2000

Struggle through the morning
in suspended
Animation feels heartless
for the chore of delving through
what comes up

next is a familiar
age old angst
before the perfume
of the day is put on

Once Again Another Century Ahead

Again.   Is this happening again?
This is the thrill of a lifetime
     once more.

Continual Conscious Compassion.

Does this include even what you don't like?
     Oh ick.

DECEMBER, 2000

To Live in this World Again

You must hide yourself
    change your flamboyance
      to a dull hue

DOES THIS MEAN I'LL NEVER HAVE ANY FUN?

No one will notice you
    The gods won't drag you off
      the earth for their own

Entertainment.   You are camouflaged
    with simplicity

2000

COLOPHON

Set in *Kennerley*, designed by Frederic W. Goudy in 1911
for the publisher Mitchell Kennerley and his edition of
H.G. Wells' *The Door in the Wall*. One of Mr. Goudy's
signature faces, it has a distinct character with roots
in the van Dyck specimens used by Bishop Fell at
Oxford University Press in 1671, a hint of Nicolas
Jenson's 1470 *Eusebius*, and kinship to William
Caslon's workhorse. With "strong serifs, firm
hairlines" this font has a sense of rolling
color on the page and almost dances
with what Clifford Burke calls
Goudy's "joyous vision."

•

Book design by J.B. Bryan

Author of over 19 books, Joanne Kyger
was born in 1934. She lives on the coast
north of San Francisco, writing poetry,
editing the local newspaper, travelling to
Mexico, and teaching frequently at the
Jack Kerouac School of Poetics at Naropa
Institute in Boulder and the New College
of San Francisco.

An active presence in the San Francisco
Bay Area poetry scene for forty years,
Joanne Kyger was one of the few women
involved with the San Francisico Renais-
sance, a constellation of writers around
Robert Duncan and Jack Spicer. One of
the acknowledged female "Beat" poets,
she has been an inspiration to countless
other writers, women as well as men,
the young as well as her peers.

photograph by Donald Guravich